ANCIENT GREEKS
WHY THEY MATTER TO US

Written by Juliet Kerrigan

CONTENTS

Collins

PART 1: WHAT'S IN A NAME?

Do you know anyone called Helen or Zoë, Jason or Alexander? These names are thousands of years old and would have been familiar to the Ancient Greeks. Have you watched the Olympic Games? Ancient Greeks would recognise them too, although their games weren't exactly the same. Have you heard the government of Britain being described as "democratic"? **Democracy** was an Ancient Greek idea. The word "idea" is Greek too!

What do these words have in common? They're all Greek.

HORIZON

DRAMA

Many of the words we use every day are Ancient Greek words, or come from Ancient Greek words. Many ideas first thought of by the Ancient Greeks have shaped the way we live our lives today.

PANTHER

ORCHESTRA

BLUE

The Ancient Greeks *didn't* have a word for the colour blue. They described the sea as "wine-dark".

ANCIENT GREECE ON THE MAP

The Ancient Greeks lived from 3000 BCE to 30 BCE in the area now known as Greece and its islands.

MACEDON

AEGEAN SEA

Delphi

Thebes

Euboea

Corinth

Athens

Mycenae

Olympia

Tiryns

Epidaurus

PELOPONNESE

Cyclades

Sparta

Pylos

LACONIA

Thera

IONIAN

SEA

Crete

ATLAS

According to Ancient Greek **legend**, Atlas was one of the **Titans**. He lost a battle against the gods of **Olympia** and, as punishment, had to hold up the sky for evermore. Early books of maps often had a picture of Atlas in them, and now we use the word "atlas" for such books.

LYDIA

NORTH
AMERICA

ASIA

EUROPE

Map area

SOUTH
AMERICA

AFRICA

)s

Rhodes

THE BRONZE AGE:
3000-1100 BCE (AROUND)

The history of Ancient Greece goes back such a long way, modern experts have divided it into different periods.
In the Bronze Age, the Minoan and the Mycenaean people lived in Ancient Greece.

THE MINOANS

On the island of Crete, people showed how important they were by building large palaces.
Four palaces, along with tombs and settlements, have been found there. Inside the largest palace at Knossos there are a hundred rooms. Some of the rooms have wall paintings: pictures of bulls and double axes. It's possible a king lived here – the one described in the Ancient Greek legend of King Minos.

In the legend, every nine years King Minos of Crete demanded a tax from the city of Athens of 14 young people. They were sent as a **sacrifice** into a maze where the Minotaur – half man, half bull – lived.

palaces of Crete

The idea of the maze in the legend could have been based on the palace at Knossos with its hundred rooms. The pictures of bulls and double axes painted on the walls may

LABYRINTH

This was the name given to the palace at Knossos, meaning "House of the Double Axe". We use the word to mean a maze.

be how the story of the Minotaur began. We don't know what the people who built these palaces called themselves, but experts have named them Minoans after the legend of King Minos.

Why these palaces fell suddenly into ruin is still a mystery. Crete may have been invaded from the mainland. Earthquakes or a volcanic eruption on the nearby island of Thera may have been responsible.

a wall painting showing people leaping over a bull for sport

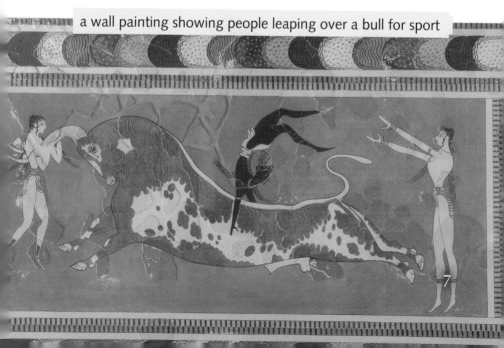

THE MYCENAEANS

Meanwhile, on the Greek mainland, cities and palaces were being built by people whom experts call Mycenaeans, after the most important site discovered at Mycenae. The Mycenaeans liked building big too. The palace at Tiryns had walls so massive that later Greeks believed that giants had built them. Clay tablets **excavated** in the best-**preserved** palace at Pylos show that the Mycenaeans could write. Daggers, gold death masks, headdresses and cups found in graves at Mycenae show these people were also expert goldsmiths.

This gold mask covered the face of a body buried at Mycenae.

Kings may have ruled from these palaces, and a polished stone block of decorated **limestone** and green marble, discovered by **archaeologists**, may have been the throne they sat on.

Just like the Minoans, the Mycenaeans **declined**, possibly because of bad harvests or earthquakes. They weren't forgotten by later Greeks who saw them as heroes who may have fought in the Trojan War.

THE TROJAN WAR

This war may have happened between the Greeks and the people of the city of Troy, which was in modern-day Turkey.

The Lion Gate is the largest Mycenaean sculpture found so far.

THE DARK AGE:
1100-750 BCE (AROUND)

When the Minoan and Mycenaean civilisations ended, all forms of writing and many of the skills of goldsmiths and builders disappeared and the style of pottery became simpler. No one knows why this happened, but it was the start of the Dark Age.

Not everything disappeared – people living in the Dark Age didn't forget about the past. Poetry **flourished** and there were many stories about the Bronze Age. A man called Homer, who may have lived around 850 BCE, **composed** a poem called *The Iliad* about the Trojan War.

a vase painting showing a scene from Homer's poem *The Odyssey*

In another poem, *The Odyssey*, Homer told of a Trojan War hero called Odysseus who spent ten years trying to return home to Ithaca. These poems were **recited** or sung from memory at special gatherings. They weren't written down until about 300 years later in 550 BCE. Dark Age poetry celebrated a glorious past which is still remembered today in films and books.

Gatherings may have taken place at Lefkandi, on the island of Euboea. Evidence of a large wooden building was discovered, and graves with jewellery, pottery and items from Egypt. There may have been more going on in the Dark Age than we think.

Lefkandi●   *Euboea*

a pottery centaur – half man, half horse – from Lefkandi, from about 900 BCE

THE ARCHAIC AGE:
750–490 BCE (AROUND)

After the Dark Age, the Ancient Greeks rediscovered writing. They also discovered new ideas. During the Archaic Age, the Ancient Greeks **navigated** their **seaworthy** boats without a compass, and explored the Mediterranean and the Black Sea. Earthquakes, shortage of water, or too many people and not enough food may have made them look for other lands to settle.

BARBARIANS

When Ancient Greeks met people who didn't speak Greek, they called them "barbarians", because their language sounded like "bar-bar-bar". Nowadays, we use the word "barbarian" to mean someone who behaves in an **uncivilised** way.

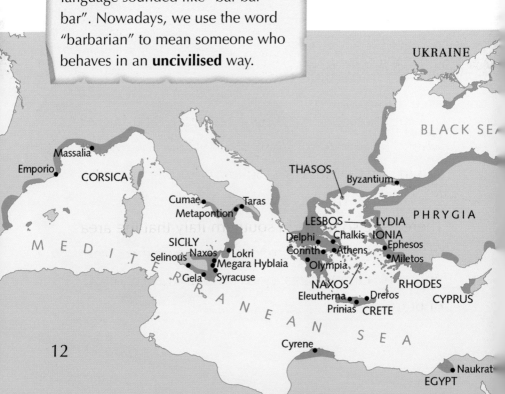

a Greek temple at
Paestum in southern Italy

They traded with people like the Phoenicians,
who lived in modern-day Lebanon, and went to
live in other countries, from modern-day Spain to
the Ukraine. These settlements were near the sea.
There were so many in southern Italy that the area
was called "Greater Greece". Wherever they went,
they took Greek ideas, gods, festivals and styles
of buildings.

The Classical Age:
490–336 BCE (AROUND)

After the Archaic Age came the
Classical Age. This was a time when
two city states became the most
important and powerful places in
Ancient Greece: Sparta and Athens.

Sparta

Those Greeks who stayed at home lived in several
city states, called "poleis". The city state of Sparta was
unlike anywhere else in Greece because the Spartans
had their own way of doing things. Two kings ruled with
a council of elders. The Spartans had large numbers of
slaves who farmed the land and had no rights.

There were no high walls around Sparta and
few remains of buildings have been found. Instead,
the Spartans had a highly **disciplined** army of foot
soldiers, called "hoplites", to defend themselves.
They trained boys from the age of seven to fight in a
group, protected by shields.

POLITICS

From the Ancient Greek word "polis", meaning "a city state", we get the words "politics" and "police".

Men and boys lived in special buildings, and the training was so tough that only the fittest survived. Soldiers wore purple cloaks and carried shields with the Greek letter L on them (after the area called Laconia).

SPARTAN

We use the word "spartan" nowadays to mean lacking in any comfort.

a marble torso of a Spartan warrior carved around 490–480 BCE

15

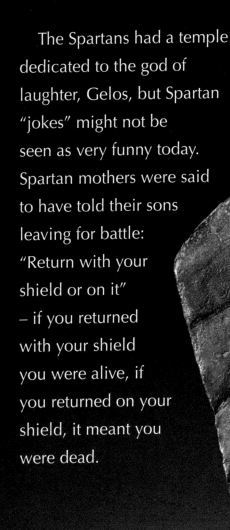

The Spartans had a temple dedicated to the god of laughter, Gelos, but Spartan "jokes" might not be seen as very funny today. Spartan mothers were said to have told their sons leaving for battle: "Return with your shield or on it" – if you returned with your shield you were alive, if you returned on your shield, it meant you were dead.

bronze statue of
a Spartan warrior

Before they went to war, the Spartans, like other Greeks, would go to a special temple where they could ask questions about the future. A priestess in the temple would give them an answer to the question, which she received from the gods. However, the answer was often in a riddle or difficult to understand. The temple, the priestess, and the answer to the questions, were known as the "oracle".

The women and girls the warriors left behind in Sparta led freer lives than those in the rest of Greece. Women could own land, and girls could take part in their own athletics.

This Spartan girl is wearing a short tunic. Women and girls in the rest of Greece wore long skirts.

17

ATHENS

Athens, another city state, was very different to Sparta.
The earliest **inhabitants** lived in safety on the Acropolis,
which is Greek for "high city". Houses, a theatre,
a marketplace and meeting area (called the "agora") were
later built on flat land around it. There were farms in
the countryside with sheep, goats and olives to provide
food and vineyards for wine. Athens became rich and
powerful – it had a big navy and there were silver mines in
the Laurium Hills.

The Athenians had a powerful
fleet of boats called "triremes".
They moved through the water at
speed, and could ram enemy ships.

PIRAEUS

The Ancient Greeks got the idea of using coins from the people of Lydia (modern-day Turkey). These coins were first made of silver and had figures, symbols and writing on them.

Athena, the goddess of wisdom, looked after Athens, and the olive tree was her gift to Athenians. Athena's temple, the Parthenon, was built on the Acropolis as one of many magnificent buildings made on the orders of an Athenian leader called Pericles about 2,500 years ago.

Coins called "owls", because they were stamped with an owl, Athena's **sacred** bird, were known all over the Greek world.

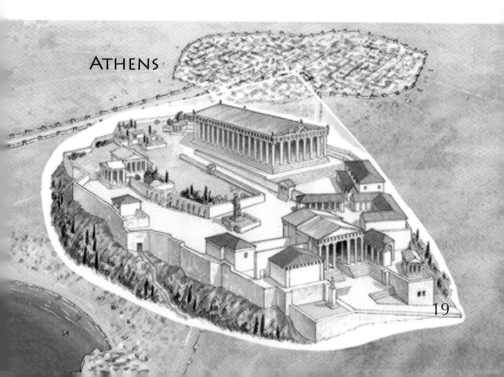

ATHENS

19

Festivals were very important in Athenian life. Every year, a procession was held in honour of Athena and a robe was specially woven for an ancient wooden statue of the goddess. There were competitions with prizes in music, poetry and athletics.

Athena was one of 12 gods and goddesses who were thought to live on Mount Olympus. The Ancient Greeks respected the gods and made sacrifices to them. Occasionally the gods helped people, but not always!

Mount Olympus

Greek Gods

ZEUS	king of the gods
HERA	Zeus's wife
APOLLO	god of the sun, music and poetry
ARTEMIS	goddess of the moon and hunting
ATHENA	goddess of wisdom
DEMETER	goddess of farming
APHRODITE	goddess of love and beauty
HEPHAISTOS	god of volcanoes, fire and blacksmiths
POSEIDON	god of the sea
ARES	god of war
HERMES	messenger of the gods
HESTIA	goddess of the hearth and family

There were other important gods too, who didn't live on Mount Olympus.

DIONYSUS	god of wine and drama
HADES	god of the underworld

Daily life in Athens

Men and boys led a free and enjoyable life – although there was always the possibility that they'd have to fight and die to defend the city. Boys were taught music, literature and physical education. By the 420s BCE, some might learn philosophy – the study of truth and knowledge – and public speaking so they could help rule. They could visit the gymnasium and take part in athletics competitions.

Women and girls led more **restricted** lives. They were expected to do all the spinning and weaving and run the household with the help of slaves. They could attend certain religious festivals and a few women might be priestesses. Girls might marry at 15, but they couldn't take part in decisions about what might happen in the city, nor visit the athletic games.

clay model of a woman kneading bread

Most Athenians wore leather sandals and simple woollen or linen tunics, with a cloak for cooler weather. Their mud-brick houses had plastered walls and earth floors, but richer families might have more **elaborate** decorations and a special dining room for the men to hold parties. They had two or three meals a day and ate bread, olives, sheep or goats' cheese, onions, celery and cucumber. Fish – fresh or dried – was a **delicacy** and meat a **luxury**. When animals were sacrificed to the gods at festivals, the meat was shared out amongst the people. Wine always had water added to it, and cakes sweetened with honey were eaten at special meals. Rich Athenians lived well!

men at a banquet

The Hellenistic period:
.336–331 BCE (around)

Alexander the Great

As the Classical Age came to an end, the Hellenistic period began and Ancient Greece, and the lands beyond, was dominated by one man – Alexander the Great. Alexander III of Macedon was one of the greatest soldiers of Ancient Greece, and the most powerful.

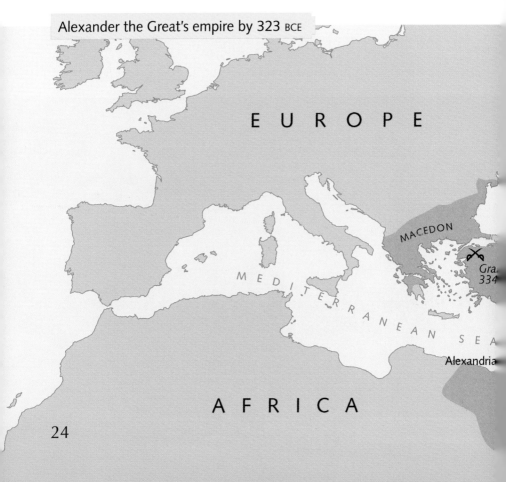

Alexander the Great's empire by 323 BCE

EUROPE

MACEDON

Gra.
334

MEDITERRANEAN SEA

Alexandria

AFRICA

Alexander's father was King Philip II of Macedon. By 338 BCE, King Philip controlled Ancient Greece and thought about attacking Persia. When Philip was murdered, Alexander became king at the age of 20. Alexander and his father's highly trained army of 50,000 men swept east as far as modern Pakistan, crushing the Persians.

an image of Alexander the Great, shown on a gold coin

Key

✗ Site and date of a battle

BLACK SEA

CASPIAN SEA

ASIA

Issus
333 BCE

✗ Guagamela
331 BCE

PERSIA

Babylon

ege of Tyre
2 BCE

✗ Hydaspes
326 BCE

In 323 BCE, Alexander returned to Babylon (modern-day Iraq), where he died aged 33 – probably of a fever, although he may have been poisoned. His amazing deeds earned him the title "The Great", but after Alexander's death, his empire fell apart.

The Romans had been challenging Greek power since the 3rd century BCE. After Alexander's death, the head of the Roman Republic, Octavian, saw his chance to expand the Roman territories, and conquered much of the land Alexander had ruled. By 30 BCE, the Ancient Greek Empire was no more.

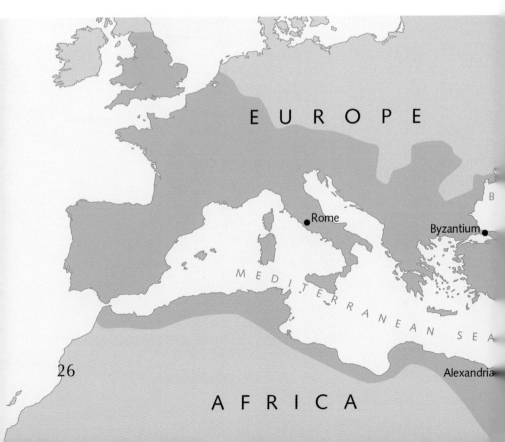

But the Romans admired much about the Greeks. They renamed the Olympian gods (the king of the gods, Zeus, became Jupiter), copied their statues and buildings, and based their alphabet on the Greek one.

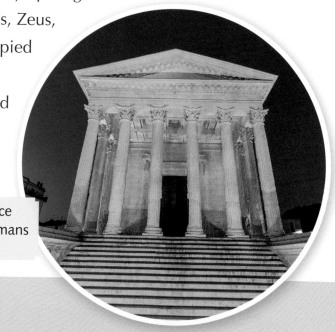

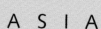
this building in France was built by the Romans in the Greek style

CASPIAN SEA

A S I A

Babylon

Land ruled by the Romans after the end of the Greek Empire

PART 2: HOW DO WE KNOW ABOUT THE ANCIENT GREEKS?

WRITING

We know about the Ancient Greeks, from the Bronze Age to the Hellenestic period, because of what they left behind. The most important thing was writing.

Some of the earliest Ancient Greek writing was found on clay tablets on the island of Crete. There were two different types of signs on the tablets. One type is known as Linear A. No one has yet been able to **decipher** what these signs mean.

Linear A

The other type of signs is known as Linear B and it dates from 1450 BCE. Experts have worked out it's a list of grain, olives, chariots and horses. It might be a list of offerings to the gods, or someone's belongings over 3,500 years ago.

Linear B

LINEAR B

Some of the marks in Linear B writing represent parts of words. For example:

a   re   i   zo   mu   wa   ra

Others are signs and pictures that represent a whole word.

man   horse   tree   helmet   wheel

It wasn't until centuries later that the Ancient Greeks, probably traders, met other traders from the Middle East, and came across a different kind of writing. This was a system of letters used by the Phoenicians. The Ancient Greeks added vowels – the letters a e i o u – to the Phoenician signs. By about 750 BCE, the earliest Greek alphabet was being used. The Greek alphabet had 24 letters, and the alphabet we use today is based on this.

Now the Greeks could write more than lists. They could have a written record of history, science, philosophy, poetry and plays, which we can study today. By the 5th century BCE, many male citizens of Athens could read and write.

ALPHABET

The first two letters of the Ancient Greek alphabet – a and b – are called "alpha" and "beta". Putting these two words together gives us our word "alphabet".

In the 5th century, everything was written in capitals. This is an inscription on the Acropolis in Athens.

BUILDINGS AND BELONGINGS

The Ancient Greeks left behind buildings – temples, tombs, theatres, palaces and houses – mostly made of stone.

Temples were built to house the statues of gods and goddesses – some of which can still be seen today. They're all built in a very similar way with stone columns in a rectangle.

Nowadays, these temples are sparkling white, but when they were first built they were painted in strong colours.

This temple is dedicated to Hephaistos, god of fire, volcanoes and blacksmiths. It has **reliefs** showing the 12 labours of Heracles – a hero in Ancient Greek legends.

The Ancient Greeks also left behind their possessions. In museums today, there are hundreds of Ancient Greek vases. Some were used for wine, some for water. They're often painted with scenes from legend, history or everyday life.

This scene from a Greek vase shows a school. The man looks like he's using a modern-day laptop. It's actually a wax tablet in a wooden case.

PART 3: WHY DO THE ANCIENT GREEKS MATTER?

Why are people who lived thousands of years ago important to us today? The Ancient Greeks had ideas that have shaped how we think now.

DEMOCRACY

Once Athens had been ruled by kings; later it was ruled by three men called "arkhons". These rulers had control over an assembly – a gathering of male citizens over 18 years old. Each of these rulers had ideas about making laws and how people lived their lives.

Experts believe that of the 40,000 men who could go to the assembly, which met every eight days, 6,000 might turn up. Although no women or slaves were allowed to be involved, the idea that so many people could have a say in the running of the city was a brand new one, which lasted about 180 years. Today, the governments of Western Europe are called democratic because adults can vote for them.

DEMOCRACY
This word comes from two Ancient Greek words: "demos" which means "people", and "kratos" meaning "power".

Name and title	Their big idea
DRACO lawmaker	In 620 BCE he drew up Athens's first list of crimes and punishments.
SOLON arkhon	In 594 BCE he made laws that gave poorer people some say in running Athens, and helped those who owed money.
CLEISTHENES leader in Athens	In 508 BCE he made sure the assembly discussed Athens, and made important decisions about the city.
PERICLES army commander and politician	In 430 BCE he said, "Our government is called a democracy because it works on behalf of the many, not the few."

Many Ancient Greeks wanted to discover how the world worked, and why.

5th century BCE
Democritus

He said the universe is made up of pieces so tiny no one can see them. He called the pieces "atomos" (Ancient Greek for "uncuttable").

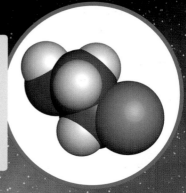

around 310–230 BCE
Aristarchus

The earth travels round the sun. This idea was forgotten for 2,000 years, but he was right!

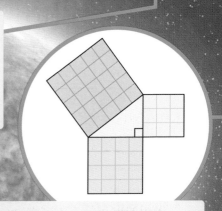

around 300 BCE
Euclid

Pythagoras's theorem (from the 6th century BCE), which Euclid wrote about, is still taught in schools today.

around 285–194 BCE
Eratosthenes

The earth isn't flat; it's round. He worked out its **circumference** as 39,625 kilometres. He was only 250 kilometres out.

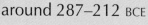

around 287–212 BCE
Archimedes

He made a **pulley** for lifting heavy objects and a screw for moving water upwards – both of these are in use today. He also worked out that a solid object forces out its own **volume** in water when he stepped into a bath, which overflowed.

EUREKA!

This is Ancient Greek for "I have found it". Archimedes shouted "Eureka!" when he stepped out of the overflowing bath.

Body and Soul – Medicine and Philosophy

Ancient Greek doctors became good at observing the signs of illness and could often tell what would happen, though treatment that worked was rare. Many doctors studied the writings of a man called Hippocrates, who'd set up a medical centre on the island of Kos. Modern doctors still make a promise (called a Hippocratic oath after Hippocrates) to treat their patients with care.

On the left, the doctor treats the young man's shoulder.

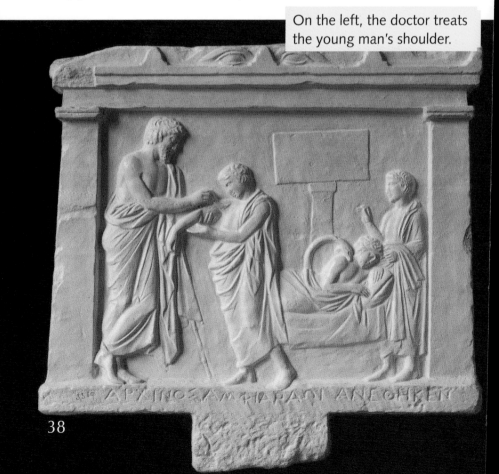

The early **philosophers** wanted to know what the world was made of and how it worked. Later philosophers looked at life differently and their ideas still influence the way people think today.

PHILOSOPHY

This word comes from two Ancient Greek words, meaning "love" ("philos") "of wisdom" ("sophia").

around 470–399 BCE
SOCRATES

He went around Athens asking tricky questions like "What is goodness?" and "What is courage?"

His efforts to make people think for themselves weren't popular. He was accused of leading men **astray** and **condemned** to death.

around 428–348 BCE
PLATO (SOCRATES'S STUDENT)

He wrote down Socrates's ideas and added his own. He thought education was very important. He also wrote about a mysterious place called Atlantis which had disappeared under the sea.

In 387 BCE, he set up a school in Athens – the Academy.

around 384–322 BCE
ARISTOTLE (PLATO'S STUDENT)

He wrote about animals, plants, astronomy, magnets, justice, politics, law, poetry and the arts.

He also found time to teach Alexander, later king of Macedon.

SCULPTURE

The very earliest sculptures we know
about came from the islands of
the Cyclades over 5,000 years ago.
Modern sculptors like Henry Moore
were influenced by them. From about
650 BCE, life-sized marble statues of
young men and women were made.
These figures had long plaited hair
and stood stiffly, often with hands
by their sides, and may have been
copying Egyptian sculptures.

This figure was made
over 5,000 years ago.

This figure by
Henry Moore
was made around
50 years ago.

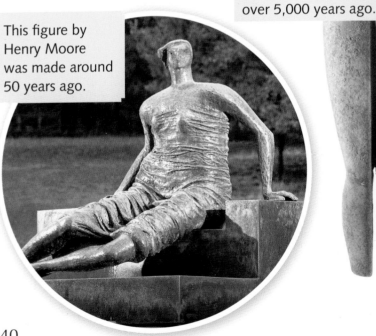

By the 5th century, figures looked more real. Many were made of bronze which was melted down and reused. Bronze figures that survived did so because they were lost at sea in shipwrecks and were later brought up by fishermen. Gods, heroes and athletes were favourite subjects. Modern scientific techniques have revealed that the white marble statues were originally painted in bright colours.

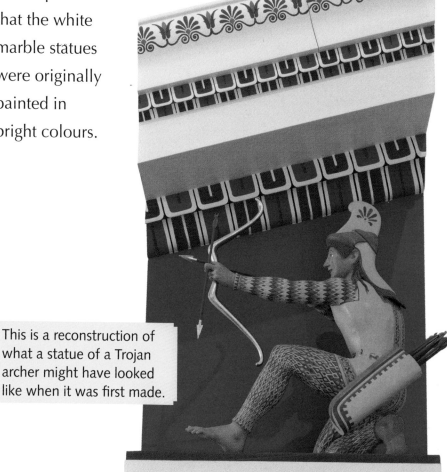

This is a reconstruction of what a statue of a Trojan archer might have looked like when it was first made.

DRAMA

All over Greece, you can still see huge open-air, semi-circular, stone theatres where thousands of people could watch plays accompanied by dancing and music. These plays were originally part of religious ceremonies. Three main actors – all men – would wear costumes, masks and wigs. A group of about 15 performers, called "the chorus", made comments about what was going on.

In Athens, playwrights took part in competitions to see whose play was considered best. Many of these plays have been lost, but surviving tragedies were tales of heroes and villains from Ancient Greek myths and history. Comedies were often about politics and recent events.

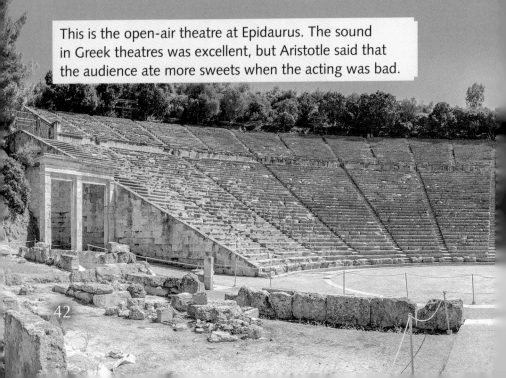

This is the open-air theatre at Epidaurus. The sound in Greek theatres was excellent, but Aristotle said that the audience ate more sweets when the acting was bad.

These plays are still performed today because they ask questions and discuss topics that we still care about: should laws always be obeyed, the fall of great men, and the effects of war.

PLAY: *Persians* (history/tragedy)   **PLAYWRIGHT:** Aeschylus

DATE OF FIRST PERFORMANCE: 472 BCE

WHAT IS THE PLAY ABOUT?: Fierce fighting between the Greeks and the Persians – the Greeks win! This is the oldest surviving Greek play. It won first prize.

PLAY: *Ajax* (tragedy)   **PLAYWRIGHT:** Sophocles

DATE OF FIRST PERFORMANCE: 444 BCE

WHAT IS THE PLAY ABOUT?: A soldier and hero of the Trojan War called Ajax.

PLAY: *Medea* (tragedy)   **PLAYWRIGHT:** Euripides

DATE OF FIRST PERFORMANCE: 431 BCE

WHAT IS THE PLAY ABOUT?: A family at war. It won third prize.

PLAY: *The Clouds* (comedy)   **PLAYWRIGHT:** Aristophanes

DATE OF FIRST PERFORMANCE: 423 BCE

WHAT IS THE PLAY ABOUT?: A play making fun of teachers in Athens and their students. It wasn't a success!

LITERATURE

Herodotus (born around 484 BCE) has been called "the father of history". He travelled around the Mediterranean looking at ancient records, collecting **eye-witness** accounts and interviewing people so that what had happened in the past wouldn't be forgotten. He believed that understanding the past was the only way to understand the present. Sometimes, if there were different versions of an event, he would include all of them so readers could make up their own minds. He wrote about the wars between the Greeks and the Persians, but also about Egypt.

HOMER

(lived around 850 BCE)
His poetry was about the Trojan War and what happened afterwards.

HESIOD

(lived around 700 BCE)
Hesiod wrote stories about the creation of the world and a golden age in the past.

THUCYDIDES

(born around 460 BCE)
He wanted to explain the present by looking at the past.
He wrote about the war between Athens and Sparta.

AESOP

We don't know details about his life, but his stories were written down around 300 BCE.
He used animal stories to point out a moral or lesson.

Sport: The Olympic Games

Ancient Greek society was the first, as far as we know, to take sport seriously. From 776 BCE, games were held every four years at Olympia in honour of Zeus, king of the gods. During the games, there was a truce: any wars were suspended. Men came from all over the Ancient Greek world to take part or watch. At first, there was only one race: the 200 metres. Other running races were added later, as well as chariot racing, and the pentathlon, which involves discus and javelin throwing, jumping from a standing start, wrestling and running. There were no team sports. Winners received a crown of olive leaves.

This bronze head of a boxer was found at **Olympia**. He's wearing an olive wreath.

MARATHON

One story says that after the battle of Marathon, where the Greeks defeated the Persians, a runner was sent over 40 kilometres to Athens with news of the victory. This is remembered in the modern Olympic Games with a running race of about 42 kilometres called the "marathon". The ancient Olympics didn't have such a race – the Greeks ran that distance not for sport but because they had to.

The last ancient Olympic Games were held around 393 CE. After a gap of 1,500 years, the games were **revived** in 1896. Today, the four-yearly Games are the world's foremost sporting event, directly

lighting the flame for the torch relay of the modern-day Olympic games

inspired by the Ancient Greeks. Men and women take part, swearing an oath just as they did at Olympia, but the carrying of the Olympic torch is a modern addition.

PART 4: DISCOVERING MORE ABOUT THE ANCIENT GREEKS

We know lots about the Ancient Greeks, but discoveries on land, and under the sea, might tell us more.

Thousands of small pieces of **papyrus** with Ancient Greek writing on them have been found on an ancient rubbish dump in the Egyptian city of Oxyrrhincus – City of the Sharp-Nosed Fish. We know there were several women poets, but only the works of one, Sappho, have survived. The writings of others – men and women – may be waiting to be found there.

Off the coast of Laconia, in southern Greece, the Ancient Greek city of Pavlopetri lies under the water. The city is 5,000 years old, but it was **submerged** over 3,000 years ago, possibly because of an earthquake. Underwater archaeologists working there may find more buried secrets from the Ancient Greek world.

ARCHAEOLOGY

"Archaeology" comes from an Ancient Greek word meaning "ancient history". It's the study of the ancient past, often using **excavation**.

The town of Pavlopetri dates back to 2800 BCE.

FROM ANCIENT GREECE TO TODAY

Writers and filmmakers today have been inspired by the Ancient Greek heroes who were given almost impossible tasks. You may know Perseus, who had to defeat a Gorgon called Medusa, and Jason, who sailed in his ship Argo to get back the Golden Fleece, guarded by a dragon.

Heroes from the Trojan War may also be familiar, like Odysseus and Achilles. As a child, Achilles, the leading Ancient Greek warrior, had been held by his heel and dipped in the river Styx to protect him. However, when an arrow hit his heel which hadn't touched the water, he died.

the warrior Ajax carrying Achilles's dead body

ACHILLES HEEL
We use these words nowadays to mean someone's weak spot.

If you met an Ancient Greek today, what sort of person would they be? They were people with open and **inquiring** minds, as can be seen from their scientists and mathematicians. They questioned authority in their pursuit of philosophy and good government. They fiercely protected their homeland, and their idea that if you have a well-trained army you can win, even if you're outnumbered, is one that hasn't been forgotten today.

Their competitiveness can be seen in their interest in sport. They were **perfectionists** in their buildings and sculptures. They expressed themselves clearly in poetry, plays, histories and writings. Life for an Ancient Greek was serious, but also to be enjoyed. These are all things the modern world can identify with.

GLOSSARY

archaeologists people who study the past using objects that have been dug up

astray go out of the right way

BCE Before the Common Era (the same as BC)

CE the Common Era (the same as AD)

circumference the distance round a circle

composed put together

condemned found to be wrong and punished

decipher find out the meaning

declined went down, became less important

delicacy special, expensive food

democracy a government in which people choose their rulers by voting for them in elections

disciplined controlled

elaborate complicated

excavated dug up

excavation a dig

eye-witness someone who saw something happen

flourished did well

inhabitants people who live in a certain place

inquiring searching for information

legend a story from the past

limestone type of stone used for buildings

luxury special and expensive

navigated directed the way a ship travels

Olympia place in Greece where the games were held (not the same as Mount Olympus where the gods lived)

papyrus tough, paper-like material made from plants

perfectionists people who want something to be excellent

philosophers	people who study philosophy
preserved	kept in a good condition and stopped from rotting
pulley	a wheel with a groove for rope to pull up objects
recited	said aloud from memory
reliefs	moulded designs or figures of people or animals
restricted	limited
revived	brought back
sacred	special to the gods
sacrifice	special present for the gods
seaworthy	good for going on the sea
submerged	went under water
Titans	a family of gigantic gods
uncivilised	rough, lacking manners
volume	space taken by a liquid

INDEX

THEN ...

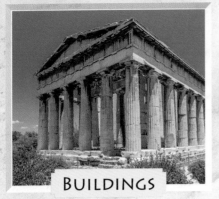

BUILDINGS

WRITING

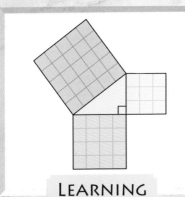

LEARNING

GREEK HEROES

THEATRE

THE OLYMPICS

... and now

Buildings

Writing

Greek heroes

Learning

the Olympics

Theatre

Ideas for reading

Written by Clare Dowdall, PhD
Lecturer and Primary Literacy Consultant

Reading objectives:
- read books that are structured in different ways
- predict what might happen from details stated and implied
- retrieve, record and present information from non-fiction
- explain and discuss their understanding of what they have read, including through formal presentations and debates, maintaining a focus on the topic and using notes where necessary.

Spoken language objectives:
- articulate and justify answers, arguments and opinions

Curriculum links: History – Ancient Greece

Resources: globe/world atlas, internet for research, drawing materials, pencils and paper.

Build a context for reading
- In pairs, ask children to build a spider diagram containing their ideas about the Ancient Greeks. Model this if necessary.
- Look at the cover, ask children *What do you think Atlas is holding?* (he is often depicted holding the Earth. The Ancient Greeks believed Atlas held up the sky). Ask children how a sculptor might represent the sky.
- Read the blurb together. Ask children to predict some ideas, discoveries and inventions that came from the Ancient Greeks. Add these to their spider diagrams.

Understand and apply reading strategies
- Turn to the contents. Help children to notice how this report-style book is organised into themed sections.
- Read pp2–3 aloud. Discuss the ideas and ask children what a democracy is. Model how to use the glossary to check the meaning of emboldened words.